What people are saying about

Past Perfect

Stephen Mitchell asks us to rethink what we mean by 'perfection', and that challenges our theology, philosophy, and notions of plain common sense. Another reader-friendly, out-of-the-box stimulant from the author of *God in the Bath*.

David Boulton, author of *The Trouble with God* and *Who on Earth was Jesus?*

Humanity's ongoing love affair with the idea of Perfection masks the self-loathing and devaluing of the everyday on which it's based. Stephen Mitchell alerts us to the perniciousness of such whoring after abstractions, and encourages us to find meaning and value in the downright ordinary – including ordinary religion. The post-modern distrust of meta-narratives couldn't wish for a more persuasive advocate of the significance of what's right in front of our eyes. A book written from a wealth of often raw personal experience, it will challenge and affirm in equal measure. Highly recommended!

Tony Windross, author of *The Thoughtful Guide to Faith*

Traditional Christianity was very pessimistic about our chances of finding lasting happiness in this life. For 'solid joys' we must seek the changeless perfection of the Heavenly World above. Stephen Mitchell's lively, original and sometimes brilliant book is a sustained attack on that idea of absolute perfection. It is also part of the process by which modern Christianity is struggling to renew itself.

Don Cupitt

Past
Perfect

Past Perfect

Stephen Mitchell

CHRISTIAN
ALTERNATIVE

Winchester, UK
Washington, USA

First published by Christian Alternative Books, 2018
Christian Alternative Books is an imprint of John Hunt Publishing Ltd.,
No. 3 East St., Alresford, Hampshire SO24 9EE, UK
office1@jhpbooks.net
www.johnhuntpublishing.com
www.christian-alternative.com

For distributor details and how to order please visit the 'Ordering' section on our website.

ISBN: 978 1 78535 788 6
978 1 78535 789 3 (ebook)
Library of Congress Control Number: 2017951276

A CIP catalogue record for this book is available from the British Library.

Design: Stuart Davies

Printed and bound by CPI Group (UK) Ltd, Croydon, CR0 4YY, UK

Contents

To Elaine
who makes my world more beautiful and loving

Past Perfect

We seem to be obsessed with perfection. It's everywhere, permeating our conversations, our language, our advertising, our films and our religion. It's not only widespread across our culture; it has roots deep in the beginnings of our civilization.

I hope to convince you that for the sake of our faith and wellbeing, we need to free ourselves from this pre-occupation. I admit to being as guilty as anyone of accepting a gift with the words "It's absolutely perfect!" but beyond such social niceties, we need to recognise that a search for perfection may inhibit our growth and sabotage any attempt to improve our lives. Equally, I certainly wouldn't want to imply that everything is imperfect since that too relies on ideas of perfection. There's no need to content ourselves with second-best, we can move beyond perfection, past perfect, embracing life, providing opportunities and creating a more just and secure world in which everyone can flourish.

From my standpoint as a retired Anglican priest, I concede that the church is similarly preoccupied with the perfect. I sing the hymn *Holy, holy, holy* with as much enthusiasm as the rest of the congregation but I know that the line "perfect in power, in love and purity" is little more than poetic alliteration.

I began this exploration after writing *God in the Bath* (O Books, 2006) in which I said that wherever we are, we are in God, for God is that in which we live and move and have our being.

> When as Christians we say we believe *in* God, it's an almost literal use of the word *in*. We believe *in* God. God is our environment, our world, our life. . . .It shouldn't therefore be difficult to believe *in* God. We shouldn't have to struggle to get our heads around impossible questions. We are already *in* God. Belief isn't like taking an exam, it's like taking a bath.

We need to learn to relax and let ourselves be revived in God's presence.

At the time I took it as understood that God embodied perfection, so was I saying that whatever it is we live and move and have our being in is perfect? When later my wife was dying of Motor Neurone Disease, it seemed an increasingly ridiculous claim to have made.

We use the words perfect and imperfect in a variety of ways to describe ourselves and the world and values such as beauty, goodness and love. However our present understanding of these is very different from that of the past, due to a huge shift in our thinking. It renders the term perfect redundant and demands a revision of our theology.

This isn't only a theological and philosophical concern, as an obsession with the perfect blights our lives in practical ways. "I am a perfectionist" people say at an interview when asked to confess their faults. It's usually a self-deprecating way of saying "I am totally committed to completing work to the highest possible standards". However, perfectionism that seeks something beyond this can inhibit creativity, leave us indecisive, and undermine our confidence. An even greater concern is that it may cost lives; research suggests that exposure to a relentless demand to be perfect, (a concept sometimes referred to as socially prescribed perfectionism), is linked consistently with feelings of hopelessness, eating disorders (particularly amongst young people), and in extreme circumstances attempted suicide.

My thanks to the team at John Hunt Publishing for their professional expertise and help. I am indebted to the late Tony Guinle, a friend, journalist and raconteur who read the first draft of these ideas with great insight and persuaded me to complete the project. My daughters, Frances and Jennifer, have been a huge encouragement, Frances challenging my thinking from her experience as a counsellor, writer and musician. Above all I want to thank Elaine who has spent many hours helping and encouraging me to produce a readable text.

Perfect Day

Nothing's perfect, they say, but it seems we are repeatedly bombarded by promises to the contrary. According to adverts on the internet, a perfect pizza, plumber, pen or pet is only a phone call away. The perfect property is just down the road. It makes the estate agent's day to unlock the front door and hear the client's "Wow!" Everyone, it seems, is looking for the wow factor. Surprise and amazement, and the recognition of beauty, ability, courage and sheer determination are all expressed in a "Wow!" as extraordinary talent, outstanding achievement, virtue, self-sacrifice or saintliness overwhelm us.

"Wow! It's perfect!" we may add. It's the perfect house with a bathroom to die for and a kitchen at the heart of the family home. Wow! But what does the "perfect" add? Are we really saying that here is something not only good, not even very good, nor even something that has the elusive X factor but perfection itself? And what is that?

Our word "perfection" comes from the Latin word *perficio* meaning to complete. The Greeks used the word *teleios* from *telos* meaning end – end that is not only in the sense of bringing something to completion but also in the sense of being directed towards a particular end or goal. It is in this way that we say the house is perfect. It's just what we've been looking for, the goal of our search. It ticks all our boxes. It's the complete package. We won't find a better one and our search is at an end. Yet while this house, with its views across the countryside and acres of ground is just right for me and my family, it isn't perfect for the young bachelor. It's not what he's looking for. Is perfect always a relative idea – perfect *for me* or *for him*?

Our everyday use of perfect reveals some other interesting and puzzling aspects of the word. Take the idea of perfection in sport, for example. In 1984, Jayne Torvill and Christopher

Dean, added to their considerable ice-skating achievements by becoming Olympic Gold medallists. The nine judges awarded them a total of 12 perfect sixes for technical aspects of the dance; the highest ever score for a single performance. However not all Olympic athletes can achieve such perfection. There are no marks awarded to 100 metre sprinters. They may win a gold medal, achieve a personal best time and even break a world record but they know that sooner or later, their record time will be broken. If they are lucky it will stand for a season or two, but sooner or later a fraction of a second will be knocked off their world record time. Excited commentators will describe them as having run the perfect race and achieved a perfect result but at the back of the athlete's mind is the thought that while they now stand on the podium listening to their national anthem, next year or the year after someone else will be standing in their place. Their achievement will be surpassed.

In Sarajevo, Torvill and Dean were also awarded a perfect six for artistic impression yet in most other artistic endeavours this is an impossible goal. Anyone who has had an essay marked will know that thoughts of perfection are discouraged. Usually a letter is given – A, B or C, sometimes in Greek – Alpha, Beta or Gamma, sometimes a classification – First, Second or Third. Even when the essay receives a mark, it is translated into letter grades: 70% to 100% is an A, 50% - 70% a B. Again the message is clear. You may be good (A), or even very good (A+). You may be excellent (A++ or A *) but you are not perfect.

Usually, in the arts, it's taken for granted that the ideal is unachievable. There's no such thing as the perfect performance or painting just as there is no such thing as the perfect crime or society and anyone who seeks such perfection is an idealistic dreamer, the target of an advertiser's campaign or victim to a politician's propaganda. Advertisers may market perfect diets and cleaning products but that's all it is, media hype.

In science, the perfect ideal has real and practical uses. The hypothetically, perfectly rigid body, the perfectly smooth surface and the perfect fluid, provide a model of how in ideal situations things behave. While they are not to be found in nature or even possible to manufacture, they provide the basis for scientific theory. Mathematicians also have a specific use for the word perfect. A perfect number - six, for example or 28 - is one which equals the sum of its divisors. (Six is the first perfect number as 1 + 2 + 3 = 6. Twenty-eight is the second as 1 + 2 + 4 + 7 + 14 = 28.) No one knows whether all the perfect numbers are even numbers or whether there are an infinite number of perfect numbers. In antiquity, Plato called 10 a perfect number. We have ten fingers! Pythagoras, claimed that six was a perfect number because our height is six times the length of our feet. Others called three and others seven perfect numbers. These are very specific, technical uses of the word perfect.

Our everyday use of the word perfect reveals another interesting characteristic.

Just a perfect day
Drink Sangria in the park
And then later
When it gets dark, we go home

What extraordinary event made Lou Read's day perfect?

Just a perfect day
Feed animals in the zoo
Then later
A movie, too, and then home
Oh, it's such a perfect day
I'm glad I spent it with you

There is nothing here to match the outstanding Olympic achievements of Torvill and Dean, and that often seems to be the case in our descriptions of the perfect. It can, we say, be experienced in ordinary, everyday activities.

What is even more extraordinary is that we talk of perfection being experienced in the imperfections of our lives. Sometimes, indeed it is the mishaps that make the day perfect. What a perfect wedding! The bride looked radiant, the service was reverent but not too formal and the reception brought both families together. Even though the groom fluffed his vows, the best man dropped the rings and it started raining as the photographs were being taken, we still say it was a perfect wedding. Indeed the unexpected mishaps made the day.

In our everyday use, perfect varies from being a simple exclamation of delight, to describing something that ticks all the boxes, suits our needs, and cannot be bettered. It describes something that is complete, the goal of our searching and, sometimes an unattainable ideal. It's used for scientific modelling and practical hypotheses. It is the name of a particular series of numbers and whereas the perfect can be seen as faultless, it can also, paradoxically, be made by accidental mishaps. This rich variation is often overlooked in our obsession with the perfect as is the joy and success that can be present in misfortune and mistakes.

There is no escape from the language of perfection in the church. God is described in the hymn *Holy, holy, holy* as "perfect in power, in love and purity". Other hymns address God as *O Perfect Love, O Perfect Redemption, O Perfect Sacrifice, O Perfect Peace.* Jesus is addressed as the perfect human being:

O perfect God, Thy love
As perfect Man did share

His disciples are called to be perfect. "Be perfect as your heavenly Father is perfect" says Jesus in Matthew's Gospel (Matthew 5.48) and if that is unattainable in this life, there's the hope of the perfection of heaven. How does this theological language relate to the everyday uses of the perfect?

Nothing's perfect, they say but of course they don't usually include God. If they do, all perfection is said to reside with God in heaven and everything, everywhere else is imperfect. Here a very clear divide is made between the perfect realised in God and our flawed, imperfect world. It leads us to ask which ways of thinking about the perfect apply to God. Is God a hypothesis, an ideal, an end of our searching, something unsurpassable? All of these have been said of God. Yet such a clear separation of the two worlds doesn't quite match Christian ideas of incarnation. Christians talk about God with us, about being made in the image of God and God's spirit being within them. They are encouraged to see Christ in their neighbour and God's will in the events of their lives and the world. If God is perfect, then Christian incarnational belief implies that something of the perfection of God is present amidst the imperfections of life. While such a paradox may excite the imagination, it may be devoid of any real meaning.

In the following chapters, I want to look at these questions by examining our use of the concept of perfection in our attempts to create beauty, love and justice and in our efforts to become better people in a better world. I believe that in these context we simply don't need ideas of perfection and moreover, therefore, neither do we need ideas of perfection in our search for the God of beauty, truth and love.

Beauty

"Out of Zion, the perfection of beauty, God shines forth," wrote the Psalmist (Psalm 50.2). Is there any perfection in beauty? Does beauty have anything to do with perfection? Is beauty a form of perfection?

There's an ancient story concerning two Greek rival artists. Zeuxis challenges Parrhasius to a paint-off to determine who possessed the greater skill. Each executes a wall painting and when it comes to the reveal, Zeuxis uncovers his first: a bunch of grapes so life-like that the birds fly down to peck at them. Confident of victory, he asks Parrhasius to remove the drape from his painting only to be told that the drape is in fact the painting. Zeuxis graciously concedes defeat.

If realistic representation is the sole aim of the painter, then artists can indeed aim for perfection in their work. Zeuxis's grapes and Parrhasius's drape would both be candidates for the perfection of beauty, but some imaginary or mythical subjects have no "original" to be copied.

There's another story about Zeuxis, in which he is commissioned to paint a portrait of Helen of Troy. He begins by looking for a model and failing to find anyone who matches Helen's mythical, spell-binding beauty, chooses five women with the intention of combining their most attractive features in his painting. Cicero, the Roman philosopher and writer, ends his account of the tale in *De Inventione* with these words.

> He chose five women because he did not think all the qualities which he sought to combine in a portrayal of beauty could be found in one person, since in no single case has nature made anything perfect and finished in every part.

We'll leave, for the moment, Zeuxis and Cicero's agreement

that nature fails to produce anything totally flawless and that, therefore, there are no perfectly beautiful women. For them a woman may have some perfect features, but other parts of her will let her down. Yet Zeuxis not only thinks that there can be perfect beauty, he believes that through his skill at mixing and matching the individual traits of his various models, he can actually bring it about in a real painting.

This may be an old story but it has uncomfortable resonances in contemporary life. Today we hear of women who are dissatisfied with their bodies. They undergo the cost and pain of cosmetic surgery in an attempt to eliminate their perceived imperfections. Nowadays the ideal for which they strive can be artificially engineered by creating computer generated pictures from a number of different components, in much the same way that Zeuxis composed his portrait of Helen. Film producers sometimes employ body doubles to compensate for nature's supposed shortfalls in parts of their leading superstars, particularly in scenes of an intimate nature. This obsession is not confined exclusively to women. Men, too, have concerns about their bodies but there is a sinister misogynist undercurrent to the old story of Zeuxis - the perfection women seek is one that is, or sometimes imagined to be, one demanded by men.

Cosmetic surgery does not always meet the high expectations of the client and can have tragic results. A more recent tale whose dénouement epitomises the very antithesis of beauty and perfection is Mary Shelley's *Frankenstein*. Its protagonist, like Zeuxis, attempts to produce a creature from various body parts and in his aspiration for the perfect form collects bones from charnel houses and scours dissecting rooms and slaughter-houses for limbs. The end result is horrific. Frankenstein's little son William utters a shrill scream on first seeing the hideous fiend. Only the blind Mr de Lacey is able to respond kindly to him. Frankenstein's later attempt to make a female companion in the hope that the loathsome creature will leave Europe for ever, disgusts him and he tears the thing to pieces.

These stories raise fundamental questions not only about our attempt to create perfect beauty but about our self-worth. If we are convinced that we and the world are in some way imperfect, we risk living in a continuing state of disappointment and dissatisfaction. If we persist in scrutinising and assessing individual physical characteristics, we adopt a festishistic, rather than holistic, approach to people.

We have another question to ask Zeuxis and Cicero and indeed Frankenstein. What are their criteria for assessing beauty? When Cicero tells us that "in no single case has nature made anything perfect and finished in every part" how is he assessing those parts he deems to be perfect? His words stand in direct contrast to Solomon who addresses his lover in the *Song of Songs* with the words "You are altogether beautiful, my darling; there is no flaw in you." (Song of Songs 4.7) Had he met Solomon's bride, would Cicero have changed his views on the possible perfectibility of nature? Would she have been the perfect model for Zeuxis' painting of Helen of Troy? Would they have seen flaws where Solomon saw none?

It has been known in certain eras for painters and sculptors to adopt mathematical criteria for the perfect form of the human body. Sculptors in Ancient Egypt followed carefully laid down rules defining the proportions of different parts of the body. Using a grid of eighteen squares, each the size of the palm of the hand, they would use the top two for the face, the next ten for the body from the neck to the knees and the remaining six for the knees to the sole of the feet. Vitruvius, living in the first century BC, in his ten volume treatise *On Architecture,* is equally clear about the proportions of the perfect human face.

> Nature has so fashioned, that in the face, from the chin to the top of the forehead, or to the roots of the hair, is a tenth part

> of the height of the whole body. From the chin to the crown of the head is an eighth part of the whole height and from the nape of the neck to the crown of the head the same.

Another ratio which the ancient Greeks found to be particularly satisfying is the Golden Ratio. A rectangle with a height of 1 unit and a width of 1.618 would fulfil this Golden or Divine Ratio. People claim to find this in the pyramids of Egypt and the Parthenon of Athens, in Chartres Cathedral and the Mona Lisa. More recently it has been claimed that the human face is perceived as beautiful if its various features are in this ratio. Stephen Marquardt, a retired maxillofacial surgeon, created an objective standard for judging the beauty of the human face. Surgeons might well use his Golden Decagon Matrix Facial Mask to help them reconstruct damaged human faces. Others may have cosmetic surgery to replicate these proportions. They may not be our criteria but if beauty is thought to have a mathematical basis, then its roots lie in a perfection that is both possible and measurable.

Not everyone sees the roots of beauty in perfection; Marilyn Monroe said "Imperfection is beauty". In contrast to Zeuxis and Cicero's aesthetic of perfection, some talk about an aesthetic of imperfection. Looking at some aspects of Japanese culture, our attention is drawn to the natural, irregular, weather-worn rocks carefully placed at the centre of a Zen garden, or to the rather rustic, imperfectly shaped tea cup which forms the focus of the tea ceremony. The outlook and approach to life that these represent is sometimes known as *wabi sabi*. In his book on the subject, Andrew Juniper says "it is these random flaws and irregularities that offer a model and humble *wabi sabi* expression of beauty". In an article entitled the "The Japanese Aesthetics of Imperfection and Insufficiency", Yuriko Saito describes *wabi sabi* as the "worship of imperfection".

The irregular, asymmetrical objects are, however, only one

aspect of this art. The rock at the centre of the Zen garden is placed within an immaculately raked sea of gravel. The tea cup finds its place within a tea house with screens and mats which are regular and symmetrically patterned.

This combination of the perfect and imperfect emerges in the following Zen story. In a distant monastery, as autumn arrives and the falling leaves begin to cover the garden, a Zen master tells his disciples to sweep the path. In the evening, the master inspects their labour. There isn't a single leaf on the path yet, to their surprise, the disciples are told to sweep it again the next day because they haven't done a perfect job. They sweep the path a second time, only to be told again that they have failed. Finally, after a third attempt, one of the disciples asks the Zen master what is wrong with their sweeping. He reaches up and gently shakes a branch. Five leaves fall onto the path. "Now the path is perfect" he says.

The falling leaves on the carefully swept path and the weathered rock set in the immaculately raked gravel hint at something else expressed through this art which is important in our consideration of beauty: the passing of time and the fragility of life. This is in contrast to the eternal images and mathematical proportions of Greek and Renaissance art, yet both aspects seem to express something of the nature of beauty on which we would focus our attention, the present moment in the passing of time, the forms and proportions which give shape to all things.

The same emphasis is found in the *Book of Ecclesiastes* where we are told "God has made everything beautiful in its time".

The writer begins the chapter by telling us there are times to weep and times to kill, times for hatred and war, but within the seasons of life, between the time to be born and the time to die, there is beauty, maybe even something beautiful in each and every season.

Imagine this conversation between two lovers.

You are beautiful.

No, you just happen to find me attractive.

No! The symmetry of your face is exact and your features are in proportion.

Nothing to do with me then! And when I'm old and my face is wrinkled, will you still find me beautiful?

I'll pay for you to have a face-lift!

Beauty seen only as the subjective delight of an individual seems to lack something enduring and objective: "*You just happen to find me attractive.*" Yet as the fulfilment of objective, formal criteria, it then ignores something essential, human and personal: "*Nothing to with me then?*" Furthermore, beauty regarded as a commodity with monetary value seems fickle and unnatural: "*I'll pay for you to have face-lift*". Beauty which is only defined by notions of perfection can lead to disappointment and despair: "*And when I'm old and my face is wrinkled, will you still find me beautiful?*"

The passing of time is an essential feature of all performance arts. A musical score only comes to life when it is performed in time. Is there a place for perfection in performance? In so far as musicians are able to fulfil a composer's intention, then it might be considered possible. Quite what those intentions are and whether they can be discovered and translated into a contemporary setting, is itself highly debatable. But in today's world of digital recording techniques with the ability to correct mistakes and enhance sounds, it might be argued that perfection is a very real possibility. Yet such a recording may take something away from the live performance which, even with inaccuracies, achieves something that no recording can ever achieve. The imperfections, some might say, make the live performance perfect.

All this brings us to yet another aspect of beauty: society's contribution and responsibility. To be part of our culture, paintings and sculptures have to be displayed in galleries, or outdoors in the landscape or the city, music and plays have to be performed on the stage and patronised and discussed by the public. For a work of art to maintain its place in the life of society, each successive generation will have to re-interpret and re-value it. There will be times when it is lost on a contemporary audience, times when it is re-discovered and finds a new relevance.

Our ideas of beauty are centred not only on particular pieces of art but within the whole creative realm of society's culture and its search for meaning and aesthetic value. Works of art and aesthetic experience are continually being renewed and redefined. It is a process without end and will go on as long as human beings seek to enhance their society through art and beauty. Notions of perfection and imperfection do not do justice to this on-going and never-ending responsibility.

There are artists today who attempt, like Zeuxis, to produce life-like images. Kelvin Okafor produces pencil drawings remarkable in being almost indistinguishable from photographs. Few, however, would say that this is the only form of painting that is acceptable or beautiful. We enjoy a rich variety of art from across the world and from many different periods of history. We also recognise that appreciation of beauty varies from one culture to another. To talk of perfection and imperfection in relation to beauty or to say that beauty is found in perfection or imperfection is to ignore the place of artistic endeavour within human life and culture and the need to assess and re-assess its value.

All this is not to say that a piece may better achieve its effect. The artist may well feel that there is room for improvement and revision. Even after the revisions, it is not helpful to refer to the work as being perfect, as it must now be displayed in the public arena. In years to come further changes may be felt necessary in order that a new audience might be similarly moved by its performance. Where life is on-going, notions of perfection are of little value. One can only hope that our aforementioned lovers will also realise that the perception of beauty is part of their on-going love for each other. While one may seek reassurance of that love from the other, to speak of a partner's beauty as perfect suggests an end of the matter rather than a continuing desire and commitment to keep love alive.

For the Christian there is a further challenging question raised by the Psalmist at the beginning of the chapter.

> Out of Zion, the perfection of beauty, God shines forth.

It also arises from many hymns that suggest that God is to be found in beauty, as in the refrain of *God is love, his the care*

> God is good, God is truth,
> God is beauty–praise him!

If God is to be found in beauty, what does our discussion of beauty say about the nature of God and where God is to be found?

Timothy Rees's hymn *God of love and truth and beauty* points in the direction of order

> God of love and truth and beauty, hallowed be thy name;
> fount of order, law, and duty, hallowed be thy name.

Is the God of beauty to be found in a theology of perfection, within that which is ordered with mathematical precision or that which fulfils our notions of logic? Is the God of beauty to be found in a theology of imperfection, in that which is unique and shaped by time and circumstance, evading precise depiction? Others will even argue for a God found in the ugly, in the fiendish and monstrous, in those rejected by normal standards. There are, for example, some extraordinarily beautiful paintings of the crucifixion by Velazquez, Caravaggio and Salvador Dali echoed in hymns like Jonny Diaz's *Beauty of the Cross*: At the cross I find the beauty of Your matchless grace.

Our discussion of beauty led us to consider our changing view of it over time and across cultures, and the role of society. All these factors make beauty something less objective and place it within our individual perceptions.

The challenge for our theology is this: If we move away from objective criteria for beauty, away from looking for beauty in perfection, towards a beauty that is subjective and in the eye of the beholder, changing over time and across different cultural contexts, should we not be admitting the same in our theology? Beauty becomes no less important for us in adopting to such a shift. We still strive for beauty in our design and creativity, it remains important to us and a reality that enhances our lives and stimulates our desires. The God of beauty becomes no less important in giving us life and value and may even become all the more real to us as our search for God becomes less objective.

Ascribing beauty is personal; it's something we do as people, it helps to define us and the things we value. To make beauty objective is to depersonalise those we call beautiful including the person of God.

Our exploration of beauty also has much to say about the process of letting go, a necessity in launching a work of art into the world. The responsibility for its future passes from artist to audience and becomes a collaboration between author, editor and reader; composer, performer and audience; lyricist, musical director, actor, producer, audience, critic and historian. As parents relinquish influence on their children and allow them to grow so must artists leave their characters and creations to find their own place in the world. Abandoning notions of perfection will help us to recognise the collaborative nature of all our endeavours and allow others to enable them to flourish. Our theology is also a collaborative effort and exploration of the God found among us.

World

Human nature aside, natural disasters and disease might be cited as ample proof of the imperfection of the world. The Christian story, as often told, seems to back this up; once everything was in perfect harmony, but The Fall, triggered by the disobedience of Adam and Eve, plunged the world back into chaos. Is there any meaning in talk of the world's perfection and imperfection?

In an episode of the award-winning series, *Inside Nature's Giants*, Richard Dawkins, standing alongside a dissected giraffe, speaks to camera.

> We get used to the idea that evolution is so good at producing beautiful, elegant animals that look as though they've been designed, we forget that sometimes they're not perfect, and there are imperfections. And the imperfections are very revealing because they are exactly the kind of imperfections you'd expect, from the accidents of history, if there were no designer.

He goes on to dissect a nerve called the recurrent laryngeal running from the larynx to the brain. Instead of simply connecting the two, a distance of a few centimetres, it loops around one of the main arteries in the chest. In the giraffe this is a considerable distance. "Obviously" says Dawkins, "a ridiculous detour, no engineer would ever make a mistake like that." If giraffes were in a position to comment, they might agree and say it is a continual bone of contention with their Creator.

Richard Dawkins is keen to demonstrate to us that the world and its creatures are not the product of an intelligent, purposeful creator, but of evolution. That is not my concern in this chapter. I am interested in his use of the word "imperfections". Had nature an intelligent designer, it would presumably be "perfect".

The accidents of nature are "imperfect" and thereby disprove a purposeful creator. We gasp in wonder at the variety of life on our planet and the awesome power of nature. Yet it is true, along with Dawkins, we rarely describe nature as perfect. If we were designing the world, besides tidying up the giraffe, we would make sure there were no earthquakes, tsunamis and virulent diseases.

The oddities of nature and the things that frustrate us, however, are not the result of the world going wrong. Natural disasters and the accidental quirks we see in natural structures are all manifestations of the forces of nature. Explicable, if not always predictable, such phenomena are simply wonders of the world. When disease strikes, terrible and painful though it may be, there is nothing wrong with nature, even if there is something wrong with us. The disease, unless attacked with invasive drugs or surgery, follows its inextricable path of destruction. Even death itself is certain and unavoidable.

So the world, as we say, is natural and when things go awry there is nothing intrinsically "wrong" within the workings of nature. Does that make nature perfect? It is, almost by definition, part of the scientific enterprise to explain without remainder, and often with mathematical precision, everything that happens. When something proves an exception to the rule, the scientist's response is not to look for a flaw in nature but a gap in their present theory. It is assumed that everything that happens will fit a pattern, however complex and however inadequately described in current scientific theory.

Richard Dawkins hasn't finished. Having pointed out the peculiarities of the recurrent laryngeal, he goes on to give us an explanation as to why it takes the route it does. Far from being inexplicable, the circuitous path of the nerve is the outcome of the giraffe's evolution.

It turns out the laryngeal nerve first evolved in fish-like

> creatures as a direct link from the brain to the gills near the heart. Fish really don't have much of a neck, so there isn't an extension to worry about in fish. It just goes directly there. Once you introduce a mammalian neck you start to get a longer neck and the heart is displaced down lower. Over millions of generations this nerve gradually lengthened. Each small step is always simpler than a major rewiring to a more direct route.

Our scientific approach to the world presumes that there are no mistakes. If a clock stops, we look for a reason; the spring has broken. Why has the spring broken? It was over-wound. Why was it over-wound? As we have already seen, when such an explanation is given for a supposed flaw in nature, our scientific theories are modified and extended. A genuine flaw in nature would have to be totally inexplicable, an utter and absolute mystery. It is hard to see how such a part of nature could ever be recognised let alone described.

In other words, science tries to explain everything and produce a Theory of Everything. When all things, without exception, have been explained then, and only then, will science have completed its task. Science will have come to an end and reached its goal and at that point might be appropriately described as perfectly describing a perfect world.

In 1931 Kurt Gödel put forward his Incompleteness Theory stating that in a closed mathematical system a complete explanation was impossible. Some argue that the Incompleteness Theory also applies to scientific theory about the physical world. Whether or not science can ever complete its task, the question as to whether that which it seeks to explain is complete is quite another matter. Indeed the very way in which scientific theory corresponds to the reality it describes is itself impossible to explain. Scientific theories may describe accurately what happens and predict what will happen, making them very powerful and extremely useful, but that is as far as they go.

Is the world perfect? Scientific research seems to presuppose that it is and works towards a Theory of Everything. Looking at the world from our own perspective, however, it would seem a little perverse to suggest that the world is perfect when so many people are suffering. The world is chaotic and hostile and it is human beings, through sheer determination and inventive technology that have harnessed its resources to enhance their transient existence. Even a few simple changes would make the world a better place for us. The world is far from perfect *for us*.

That we can imagine a world with fewer obstacles and life-threatening challenges does not necessarily imply that such a world is a feasible reality. One morning, driving away from home, I scraped my car on the gate post. Why today, I wondered? I've done it a hundred times without a problem. In a perfect world I would not have hit the gatepost. Of course, it makes sense to say I could have driven off without an accident. Yet for that to be a real possibility, I have to know everything about the car and the conditions on that particular morning as well as my own physical state and mental condition. It may turn out that there was a defect in the steering mechanism which caused the car to swerve. I may have had a sudden spasm causing me to turn the wheel at the wrong moment. I may have been distracted by the thought of something I had to do that day. These begin to sound like lame excuses for careless driving! Yet to make the move from saying "I can imagine this" to saying "therefore it is a real possibility" demands I have a full and complete knowledge of the situation.

We can imagine a world where people do not feel pain and where there are no volcanoes and tsunamis. It is a logical and coherent idea but to go on and say that such a world is a real possibility demands that we have a complete knowledge of the circumstances. By what processes could such a world have come about? What changes to the laws of geophysics would have created a world liberally supplied with fresh water? What would be the consequences for the rest of nature of such geophysical tweaks? Today we look upon the processes of our planet as being part of a single system. A change to one of those processes has far-reaching consequences for the whole system. Are other such worlds possible and would they be suitable environments for human beings? We cannot be confident of ever gaining the complete knowledge needed to answer the question. We can say that if everyone in our world is to have access to fresh water, fertile soil and painless teeth, we will have to bring it about through our own efforts. To be more precise, it will come about through the processes of evolution which have produced human beings able to shape their environment.

To summarise: first, science tends to acknowledge that there are no faults or flaws in the world as it exists and seeks to explain everything by consistent and universal laws. Second, we can imagine worlds more suited to human life and while they may be coherent and prove an inspiration for film-makers and novelists, and even though we strive to bring them about, it is difficult to know whether such idealistic environments are genuinely possible without human intervention.

We find ourselves in an awesome universe which fills us with wonder. It excites our curiosity and has led us along a scientific path to an ever-expanding human resource in the search for knowledge. Our exploration of the world assumes that it is a complete system without exception, yet our understanding of it may never be complete. Our imaginative play with the world assumes that the world could have taken on a multitude of different forms, some much more congenial to human needs. Paradoxically, our ability to conceive such worlds is matched by an inability to declare them feasible or viable without human intervention. It seems therefore that there is little to be gained in attributing notions of perfection or imperfection to our world. We should move beyond such descriptions and continue to explore, explain and exercise our creativity within it.

The design argument, which Richard Dawkins is keen to refute, the argument that tries to show that the ordering of the universe is evidence that it was created by God, is probably as old as philosophy itself, yet it is still fiercely in contention today. Creationism and Intelligent Design are pitted against Evolutionary Science in a battle which has even been fought out in the courts. It's an argument that focuses on the perceived perfection and imperfection of the world. Refusing to attribute these notions of perfection to the world can help us move away from fruitless discussion.

Traditional Christian talk about the creation moves us in the same direction. For Christians the creation isn't a one off event in the past but an on-going process. Moreover God doesn't make the world out of pre-existing material but out of nothing. Everything is utterly dependent upon God. The question "Who made the world?" doesn't therefore get us to heart of God. "Who makes the world?" or "What makes the world go round?" are questions of more religious significance.

There is a further crucial aspect to Christian teaching about creation. Looking around the universe we see tables and chairs, planets and stars but nowhere will we stumble across God. God is not just another thing that exists, in fact not a being at all. Aquinas (in *Summa Contra Gentiles* 2) proposed that this could be expressed by saying that God is "beingness itself". We might attempt to put it another way by saying that God is not a thing, but "thing-ness itself", more poetically we might say God is not alive but "life itself" or even more controversially, not real but "reality itself".

So much discussion about the perfections and imperfections of the world is a religious distraction. A search for God in the ordering of the world will be as frustrating as our search for perfection in nature. The universe is awe-inspiring; so too is our ability to describe and explain it and the use of our knowledge to transform our lives. Our search for God is better directed through those feelings of awe and in that which motivates us to transform the world and be creative within it. Our search for God is better found in our acceptance of all life, in its various forms, for the God of life, as the hymn *Holy, holy holy* says, is in all life.

To all life Thou givest, to both great and small;
In all life Thou livest, the true life of all.

Humanity

In one of the creation stories of the *Book of Genesis*, God creates human beings and places them in the Garden of Eden. Here, before Adam and Eve eat the fruit from the Tree of Life, harmony exists between all life on earth. From a later period, the prophet Isaiah presents a similar vision.

> The wolf also shall dwell with the lamb, and the leopard shall lie down with the kid; and the calf and the young lion and the fatling together; and a little child shall lead them. And the cow and the bear shall feed; their young ones shall lie down together: and the lion shall eat straw like the ox. And the sucking child shall play on the hole of the asp, and the weaned child shall put his hand on the cockatrice' den. They shall not hurt nor destroy in all my holy mountain. *(Isaiah 11.6)*

Isaiah's child reminds us of Mowgli . "The more I learn what is a man, the more I want to be an animal" he says in the 1967 film *The Jungle Book*. Brought up from an early age by a pack of wolves, his re-introduction into British "civilization" in India is painful and disorientating. "I am not a man! [pause] And I am not an animal."

Fascination with wolf children goes back at least to the time of the myth of Romulus and Remus and the theme still haunts us, judging by the many hoax accounts written of feral children today. Equally appalling are the accounts of children severely abused by adults and kept imprisoned and deprived of human contact sometimes for many years.

Our interest in these cases is sustained by the question as to what constitutes being human. Although we have a common biology with all animals, our human nature is not innate but acquired through the society, language, customs, life-styles and the traditions of our cultures. Evidence from wolf-children suggests that if some of this is not learnt at an early age, it can never be learnt.

Far removed from Mowgli is the Six Million Dollar Man, the hero of a long running and successful American television series of the 1970s. When Steve Austin is severely injured in a test flight accident, his superior, Oscar Goldman, is determined to give him a new life.

> Gentlemen, we can rebuild him. We have the technology. We have the capability to make the world's first bionic man. Steve Austin will be that man. Better than he was before. Better, stronger, faster.

Upgraded, the Six Million Dollar Man has an eye with a zoom lens and night vision, bionic legs enabling him to run at the speed of a car and an arm with the crushing strength of a bulldozer. How the rest of his body manages to support the enormous weights upheld by the bionic arm is never explained!

The culture that helps to mould our humanity has also inspired its technological advances and today such cyborg improvements are far from fictional. Visual cortex and cochlear implants are already giving patients a degree of sight and sound. Restoring damaged senses might only be a beginning in terms of further enhancing our human faculties. In 2002, Kevin Warwick, a British scientist working at Columbia University, New York, had a neural implant which enabled him to connect his nervous system to the internet. From the United States he was able to control a robotic arm in the University of Reading, UK, and to obtain feedback from sensors in its finger tips. More remarkably, his wife also had an implant secured to the nerves in her arm enabling the couple to communicate directly through their nervous systems. In 2017, Bill Kochevar, who had been paralysed for eight years, had electrical implants fitted into the motor cortex of his brain and sensors inserted in his forearm. These allowed the muscles of his arm and hand to be stimulated in response to signals from his brain, enabling him to drink and feed himself without assistance.

Enhancing the capabilities of the human body raises serious ethical issues. Since the 1980s, human growth hormones have been given to children whose hormone deficiency makes them much shorter than average. This is generally felt not only to be acceptable but also desirable; however, the use of those same hormones for the purpose of creating a "super-race" of above average-height, world-class basketball players, for example, might be considered wholly unacceptable and with regard to their sport tantamount to cheating.

Even if the application of pharmacological advancements, in a sporting, as opposed to a medical context, is not thought to raise moral issues, it gives rise to a more considered definition of the word "sport". In the 1981 film *Chariots of Fire*, the Master of Trinity College, Cambridge criticises one of the runners for employing a professional coach with accusations of ungentlemanly and tradesman-like conduct. Today, in most sports even with a great many technological and coaching aids, we still wish to celebrate personal talent and achievement, dedication and hard work. No doubt watching genetically enhanced humans competing would be as exciting as watching the popular TV show, *Robot Wars* but something would have been lost from the ethos of sport as we have understood it in recent generations.

The engineering of human beings by means of genetic enhancements could have and has had devastating implications. Historically there has been evidence of an almost duty-bound compulsion to widen the range of human capabilities. Sir Frances Galton, a relation of Charles Darwin, made the case for genetic enhancement at the end of the 19th century.

> What nature does blindly, slowly, and ruthlessly, man may do providently, quickly and kindly... The improvement of our stock seems to me to be one of the highest objects that we can reasonably attempt.

Enthusiasm for the science of eugenics (meaning *good birth*) in the 1920s and 30s, when the movement was well-established in America and Germany, led to forced sterilization programmes. In Nazi Germany, The Law for the Prevention of Hereditarily Diseased Offspring in 1933, introduced compulsory sterilisation of any citizen who according to the opinion of a "Genetic Health Court" suffered from a list of alleged genetic disorders. By the late 1930s, the Nazi government was using propaganda films to persuade the public that those who were hereditarily ill and, therefore, dangerous to the health of the nation should be exterminated rather than kept alive as "neutered beings." Under Hitler, this prejudice and fanaticism led to mass murder and genocide.

Even in a more benign society, parents might feel obliged to select (if it were possible) their children's height, sex, sexual orientation, IQ or athleticism as well as freedom from many diseases. Not giving their children every genetic advantage might be considered negligent or seen as a failure to provide fully for their future success and fulfilment. More importantly, their children's sense of autonomy and freedom would be severely compromised. To a great extent we perceive our lives as a gift, something bequeathed to us by nature, chance or God from which we seek to make something of our lives. Where life is artificially designed by parents, then the obligation to them might remain for ever. Removing all contingency from human life denies subsequent generations the privilege of self-determination which, in spite of the risks and dangers involved, must be ranked among the most challenging and ultimately rewarding of human aspirations.

Another advantage of leaving our potential talents and abilities to chance at birth is that it engenders a sense of humility regarding our significance in the "grand scheme". Where everything is designed and human beings are entirely self-made there is little room for humility, nor much opportunity for taking responsibility for our lives or those of others; if we feel that good fortune has come our way by accident rather than design, the chances are we will recognise this unearned advantage and look to support those less fortunate.

Transhumanists predict that enhancing human beings will be so radical as to make them post-human. Kevin Warwick, in an answer to questions about the future of human beings said

> Those who want to stay human can and those who want to evolve into something much more powerful with greater capabilities can. There is no way I want to stay a mere human!

In generations to come, as life on earth becomes more hazardous and resources become scarce, human beings, they imagine, will break away from their biological limitations and having uploaded their minds to super computers, will make their home in distant galaxies.

Ray Kurzweil, in *The Singularity is Near: When Humans Transcend Biology* looks forward to the fulfilment of the following predictions

> 2010s Cell phones will be built into clothing and will be able to project sounds directly into the ears of their users.
> 2020s Virtual reality will be so high-quality that it will be indistinguishable from reality.
> 2030s Mind uploading becomes possible.
> 2040s People spend most of their time in full-immersion virtual reality
> 2050s The sharp distinction between humans and machines

will no longer exist thanks to cybernetically enhanced humans and uploaded humans.

Whether this will ever be technically possible is debatable but transhumanists argue that advances in genetics, nanotechnology, robotics and artificial intelligence will together bring about a singularity-future, the limits of which may be impossible to predict.

These sci-fi scenarios not only raise questions as to what it is to be human, but what sort of environment is most conducive to human existence and survival. Those who envisage a human life in a perfect relationship with the environment present two equally persuasive scenarios; the nostalgic idyllic paradise and the futuristic technological utopia. In an attempt to live with and according to the rhythms and cycles of nature, many work towards recovering a Mowgli-like sense of unity with the natural world and the lost skills of our ancestors. For others, however, the future lies in surviving within the virtual reality of a technological bubble.

Whether one looks towards a future in harmony with nature or a one of a designed humanity, both worlds would require extraordinary technological advances. As the name implies, there is nothing natural about the Garden of Eden; it is a carefully cultivated and managed environment, no less organised than one created to a more sophisticated "virtually real" model. And can such visions of the future be described as perfect?

The Garden of Eden, though often portrayed as a place where everything is in perfect harmony, is a curious place. Without other human beings, without children, with no political or social challenges, there seems little to test that peace. We are left to speculate on what sort of life Adam and Eve might lead but without social interaction it would be a less than genuinely human life. The same could be said of the virtual world of the transhumanists uploaded minds. As far as we can appreciate, human minds require physical bodies. It is not altogether clear what could actually be uploaded to a super computer but in no sense could it be described as human.

In the previous chapter, we argued that even though the world is not always comfortable for us and even when there is something wrong with us, there is nothing wrong with the world. There is no flaw in its workings. Here too we confront fact that painful and frustrating as it might be, the environment we find ourselves in is the one which enables human life to flourish. To be human is to explore, to be social and political, and to be imaginative, brave and loving. Furthermore we are creatures of technology, shaping our environment and in so doing also shaping ourselves. Such powers seem almost God-like.

We live our lives through our bodies which in turn relate to their environment. Our capacity to shape that environment and modify our bodies is greater than ever before. Yet it seems that the relationship will be constantly changing. Any talk of perfecting either ourselves or our world makes little sense and attempts to perfect them through technological and genetic enhancement, risk losing the humility, solidarity and responsibility that we consider valuable and essential to human life.

This is the life in which we can fulfil our human hopes and become children of God. The challenges we face to sustain our environment and create peace are immense. It makes no sense to describe it as perfect or imperfect. Affirming our life is not helped by imagining a perfect world in the past or the future. In the story of creation, God declares the world to be good. That should be good enough for us.

Goodness

A tale of my father's recalled from childhood is that of a French Horn player who found God. The war had sadly brought the local amateur orchestra's music-making to an end and some years later my father set out to revive it. The horn player, meanwhile, had joined the local Christadelphian Church and when asked if he would return to the brass section said that now that he was a Christian, all his time was to be devoted to doing "good works". This did not impress my father one jot; in his eyes, a major prerequisite for leading the life of a committed believer was not immediately to offer up one's hobbies on the altar of self-sacrifice.

It is not unusual for us to forsake something in order to pursue a goal we feel to be more worthwhile. When the sacrifice is extreme, we admire such dedication and I'm sure my father had great respect for the time and effort needed to learn the French horn. So why was he uneasy about making a sacrifice for faith? My father was not opposed to Christianity; he was a churchwarden at the local parish church and the denomination his friend had joined was neither strict nor oppressive. What irked my father was not the discovery and pursuit of a faith in itself but the abandonment of everything else purportedly for faith's sake. He felt something essential to the man's character and humanity was being lost.

If there's one thing God is said to be it is good, not just good but perfectly good. The same is said of Jesus – the only perfectly good man. It's an image we have of the saints and something Christians often feel they should strive for. Yet as my father discovered, someone totally given over to doing good makes us not only suspicious of them but wonder at the very idea of perfect goodness.

In an article entitled *Moral Saints* in the *The Journal of*

Philosophy (Vol. 79, No 8 1982), Susan Wolf argued that people whose every action is as "morally good as possible", would be so taken up by their commitment to feeding the hungry, healing the sick and raising money for charity that they would have no time or energy left for "reading Victorian novels, playing the oboe, or improving their backhand." Nor could they use any of their money or resources to enjoy gourmet food or fine arts. Moral saints would have to root out personal traits such as a cynical or sarcastic wit and be unfailingly considerate and inoffensive in every aspect of their life. This, in her view, would make them dull-witted, humourless and bland! Wolf concluded that while "it *is* morally good to be a moral saint, a moral saint is not a good kind of person to be and the life of a moral saint is not a good life to lead." There are other desirable qualities, "non-moral virtues", needed if we are to be rounded characters.

In other words, Wolf distinguishes between general ideas of a good person living a good life and the more limited view of pursuing moral goodness. Of course, not everyone can be an accomplished horn player or a top-ranking tennis player, but leading a satisfying, balanced life will surely involve pursuing some such activities even though, in the case of playing an instrument, the fruits of those labours may not bring as much satisfaction to the general public as to the participant!

Susan Wolf then explores what might lead people to be moral and asks us to imagine different kinds of good people. First there are those who quite naturally and with no effort respond to everyone and every situation with a willingness and desire to do good. Others, however, might find the business of becoming a moral saint a great challenge in which they are constantly fighting the temptation to give time to their own pursuits or even to do reprehensible things. Which of these two is the better person? The first type of moral saint, whose default position is simply to do good, will never think of being vindictive. Committing a vindictive act would never cross their mind whereas the second type of moral saint may have a very strong urge to cause harm, but by strength of will manages to overcome the temptation. The outcome is the same; both act in the best possible way but we would probably admire the second kind of moral saint above the first as the second demonstrates real courage and determination. Indeed in the first case it is hard to see whether there was anything *morally* praiseworthy: they couldn't help but do the right thing.

The first moral saint may have had to work very hard for their selflessness to become second nature. This, then, gives three kinds of moral saints – one that is and always has been selfless and always, without fail, will do what is best; another who has worked hard to achieve this position; and a third who while always doing good is still battling with temptation in order to achieve it.

Now, which of these three, asks Wolf, do we admire most? There is a reluctance to elevate the first because it is simply not in their nature to do anything other than to behave in an exemplary manner. We do not attribute moral worth to a calculator for giving the right answer. That is what it does. The second who has worked hard to reach the state of the first is to be admired for the effort involved in achieving that state. However, in so far as they are now programmed to do good they are no better than the first. The third character remains most worthy of our respect, in that they experience the strongest temptations to break the moral code, yet through strength of character, courage and clear thinking as to the consequences of their actions they do what is best.

Interestingly none of the three saints achieves perfect goodness. The much admired third type of moral saint, even though they always do what is right, cannot really be described as perfectly good since they entertain and are tempted by wrong actions. As we usually associate being good with being praiseworthy, the first and second saints are also ruled out.

As we have seen they always act in the best possible way but because they never entertain doing anything other than good they are not therefore particularly praiseworthy. A moral saint not only fails to achieve a rounded character, but fails to achieve perfect goodness!

Wolf's description of a moral saint is someone whose "every action is as morally good as possible". The phrase "morally good as possible" is not without difficulties. Even distinguishing helpful from harmful actions is not easy. In the story of the Good Samaritan in Luke's Gospel, a man is attacked by robbers and left for dead at the side of the road. Two men pass by on the other side while another, a Samaritan, stops, dresses the man's injuries, puts him on his donkey and takes him to a nearby inn. Passing by on the other side is not very charitable but, as is often pointed out, binding up the wounds and lifting the injured man on to a donkey is not without risk. If the Samaritan's actions caused additional injuries, such as infecting the wounds or damaging the man's back, we would conclude that he would have been better left. Going to fetch expert help would have been a more considered course of action. Yet the Samaritan could not know that his oil and bandages would introduce infection. He could not know that his donkey would throw the man to the ground causing paralysing back injuries. The element of risk in our actions and the element of luck influencing their consequences prevent us from knowing which will prove to be the best possible decision.

Defining the best possible moral action is not at all straightforward. Is the one which produces the best outcome, or is it one in which we follow laid down moral rules or adhere to given moral values, whatever the consequence? As we see in the parable of the Good Samaritan, outcomes are not always predictable and may depend very much on luck and the decisions that other people choose to make. A person may take what turns out to be the best course of action but that may have less to do with their own moral judgement and more to do with the decisions of others and a fortunate turns of events.

A person may be commended for their action because they are said to have "done what is right" or "done their duty" or acted from the best of motives, but good intentions and values do not guarantee a happy outcome. "His heart was in the right place", we sometimes say, when things go wrong. If that person, however, acted without proper consideration of the risks and consequences involved or without taking necessary precautions, we may wonder quite where their heart was and whether they would have been better advised to step aside and allow those better qualified to deal with the situation.

Often we face conflicting values when making decisions. Should we tell our friends the truth, and risk offending them? Is it right sometimes to lie to protect someone from harm? Is it right to hurt or even kill in self-defence? The best we can do in some circumstances is the lesser of two evils and though the result may satisfy no one, it may be the preferable option, even if one of the consequences is to cause acute pain and suffering. Few of us in these circumstances would pat ourselves on the back saying we carried out the best possible action and were morally perfect.

Susan Wolf's moral saints are evidently acting autonomously which is a position we all find ourselves in at times and can be a lonely business. Very many decisions, however, are made within families and communities and issues of health, welfare and business are more often taken by statutory, professional or interested bodies. It is the responsibility of these groups to seek out the wishes of all the people affected by the decision. While we hope that they will put aside self-interest out of a commitment to all those concerned, we also want the members of decision-making bodies to be good committee members, able to listen to others and put aside personal prejudice as well as being politically astute, able to argue their point of view and convince people of a need to change. The chair of these agency committees will require skills which enable members of the group to communicate with one another and come to a decision. The qualities necessary for people to take effective action in these circumstances are wide-ranging.

Doing good in our world, bringing about improvements in our society and in our own lives is a complex and on-going business. It is tempting to look to an ideal of perfect goodness and perfectly good people to inspire and encourage us. Yet when we try to give an account of the perfectly good action we find ourselves facing an impossible task. Not only are we faced with a host of possible consequences resulting from our actions, we find ourselves having to decide between a wide variety of competing claims as to what the best possible action might be. When we try to imagine a perfectly good person, either we picture someone whose perfection robs them of humanity and effective moral character or someone whose inner struggle leads us to see them as anything but perfect, even though they might be wholly admirable in their endeavours.

It should hardly surprise us that novelists have found it a challenge to create characters of the utmost goodness; Dostoevsky in his novel *The Idiot* set out, in his own words "to depict a completely beautiful human being". He faced the problem that all morally incorruptible characters face in literature - virtue in fiction is simply not as interesting or compelling as wickedness, and runs the risk of repelling readers since it reeks of sanctimony and a lack of common humanity. Goodness also tends to align itself with unselfishness which on one level dilutes the potency of sexual energy between characters, another great driving force in fiction. So the central character, the idiot, the "good" Prince Myshkin, in spite of his best intentions, adversely affects the lives of those around him, and ultimately achieves nothing.

According to Jesus' summary of the law, the second great commandment is "Love your neighbour as yourself." We should be encouraged by this to pay as much attention to ourselves and our own development as human beings as to charitable works. At the same time, in the parable of the Good Samaritan, Jesus commands his enquirer "Go and do likewise". We are called to be ready and willing to step aside from other tasks, even from fulfilling our duty to ourselves or others, and respond to the crisis in our midst. Again we should be encouraged that the meeting of one challenge will leave others things undone, yet responding to need involves risk - risk of making things worse, risk of failure, risk of having our efforts thrown back in our face.

As Christians we cannot ignore a further command of Jesus in the Sermon of the Mount: "Be perfect as your heavenly father is perfect" but we can ask what is being demanded of us. Some claim this is an impossible ideal which we must strive towards. Others have said that we cannot achieve this by our own efforts but is granted to us by the grace of God. It's a question Charles Wesley wrestled with in his book *Christian Perfection* and throughout his ministry. He believed – in a way that reminds us of Susan Wolf's second type of Moral Saint – that God's loving grace could transform our lives to the point where our love for God and others becomes a "natural" response. Some of his Methodist colleagues believed this could be achieved within the lifetime of the believer, even immediately. Others, as Wesley himself began to believe, through more gradual growth to maturity.

If we feel compelled to use this language of perfection, then we must at least be clear as to what it means. It does not mean being a Moral Saint which as we have seen is impossible and neglects the call to be human. It does not mean doing the right thing in every circumstance, since that is impossible to define and ignores the risks involved in any course of action. Nor are we called to ignore the inevitable conflict of duties that arise and results in a failure to complete some obligations. We are called to be human, to wrestle with the all the complexities of action, to respond spontaneously to need and risk failure and abuse for our efforts. And we are called to love.

Love

On the anniversary of my wife's death, I lit a bonfire to burn the letters of our courtship in respect of her wishes and by way of a symbol of moving on, and as each was shredded and committed to the flames, I wondered how many times the word love appeared in the correspondence. I rescued from the fire two little books, no more than a few centimetres square, full of sayings and poems about love. "Love is all we have, the only way that each can help the other" wrote Euripides, a 5th century BCE Greek playwright. "Love is, above all, the gift of oneself" (French playwright, Jean Anouilh). "Love is the greatest refreshment of life" wrote Picasso - page after page of quotations. The hymnbook too is full of lines on love "Love divine, all loves excelling" "O perfect love, all human hearts transcending". What did they add up to? What is love? Are there any aspects of love that could give sense to the idea of perfect love?

We know what it isn't. As St Paul writes in his *First Letter to the Corinthians* "Love is not jealous or boastful; it is not arrogant or rude, does not insist on its own way; it is not irritable or resentful; it does not rejoice in wrong." We know some of the signs of love: "Love is patient and kind", but what is it "that bears all things, hopes all things, believes all things, endures all things" and without which we are noisy gongs and clanging cymbals?

Love, of course, is not a thing but an aspect of the way we relate to people, the world and the things we do. I love my job. I love England. I love my children. All these express our delight and commitment, but do they have anything in common? C. S. Lewis in his book *The Four Loves* describes the full spectrum of love from the simple pleasures of life to our friendships and passions and a self-sacrificing, divine love. Yet, as he observes, these loves merge into one another and are not always easy to distinguish.

Our loves range from the madness of passionate affairs and impossible and unrequited loves (some of which end tragically), to life-long commitments over sixty years of friendship and marriage. They too may end in bittersweet partings. Love occupies our minds and demands a great deal of attention. It is the subject of countless conversations, novels, films, poems, operas and soap-operas. Being such an all-embracing term, and being so fundamental to our relationships and sense of well-being, it should not surprise us if it defies definition. We naturally and spontaneously tell our children that we love them and yet struggle when confronted with the lover's question "Why do you love me?" What is love? How do we justify particular loves; indeed can they be justified? There would seem little sense in talking about *perfect* love if we cannot improve our understanding of the fundamental concept.

In everyday conversation, when we talk about loving our work or our pets we are saying little more than that we like or value these things. When we talk of loving our friends, children or partners, we are speaking of something more personal and infinitely more complex. We may like our partners very much but loving them expresses something deeper. The problem comes in trying to identify what it is that gives this "depth" to love.

Accounts of love tend to centre around four main ideas. The first is that in loving someone we form a union with them. It is well expressed in *West Side Story* when Tony and Maria sing "Make of our hands one hand, make of hearts one heart, make of our lives one life". This sense of oneness often springs from the passion and intimacy of a sexual relationship. As "my" concerns and "your" concerns become "our" concerns and what I desire becomes what we desire, separate identities become a shared identity. As the Persian poet, Farid Al-Din Attar, writes in *Intoxicated by the Wine of Love* from *The Jawhar Al-Dhat*

> In love no longer "Thou" and "I" exist, for self has passed away in the Beloved.

There is, however, something rather unsettling in this definition, for to be a person is to be an individual with distinct characteristics and an independence and autonomy. Love understood as a union undermines this individuality and may therefore be considered too restrictive and binding. These concerns are expressed in a passage from *The Prophet* by Khalil Gibran which is often read at marriage services.

> Love one another, but make not a bond of love:
> Let it rather be a moving sea between the shores of your souls.
> Fill each other's cup but drink not from one cup.
> Give one another of your bread but eat not from the same loaf.
> Sing and dance together and be joyous.
> But let each one of you be alone,
> Even as the strings of a lute are alone though they quiver with the same music.
>
> Give your hearts, but not into each other's keeping.
> For only the hand of life can contain your hearts.
> And stand together yet not too near together;
> For the pillars of the temple stand apart.
> And the oak tree and the cypress grow not in each other's shadow.
> Let there be spaces in your togetherness,
> And let the winds of the heavens dance between you.
> Love one another, but make not a bond of love.

While interdependence and mutual support may well be an important aspect of love, quite what the status of this bond is and whether to talk of a union as anything but metaphorical, is less clear.

A second view of love adopts as its defining feature that of concern. We care for and are concerned about those we love. I want my children to be happy and am concerned for their well-being. When things go well for them, I am happy and when their worlds fall apart, I am devastated. It is summed up by Thomas Merton in *No Man is an Island*:

Love seeks one thing only: the good of the loved. It leaves all the other secondary effects to take care of themselves.

This commitment of care forms part of the marriage vows "to love and to cherish 'til death us do part". This view too is not without its critics for it seems to suggest that love aims for a particular end, the good of the beloved. Yet often we speak of love as our delight in people as they are, and those we love may complain that they want us to love them whatever the circumstances. If no good is to be had and worse is yet to come, we hope our love will remain constant "for better or worse, for richer or poorer, in sickness and in health". A love that is only concerned with a person's happiness and prosperity appears to ignore the very personal attachment at the heart of loving relationships. Morally, it may be argued, I should be concerned and care for all those I meet whether I have a particular liking or affinity for them or not. Equally we talk about loving the most irksome members of our family, people we may not particularly like or for whom we have no strong feelings of concern.

A third understanding of love centres on the value of a person, appreciating them and responding to their valuing of us:

> I love you not only for what you are, but for what I am when I am with you. I love you not only for what you have made of yourself, but for what you are making of me. I love you for the part of me that you bring out. (Robert Croft: *Love*)

Again this seems straightforward but becomes more difficult

when we consider that although we might respect people we meet for their qualities and individuality, love is far more selective. We don't fall in love with everyone we meet and with all those we respect. There must be more to love than the appreciation and response to the worth and dignity of a person. A second concern is that we expect love to be constant. Where love is seen as valuing a person's qualities, reasons can be given to justify such love but if this forms the essence of love, then were those qualities to change, so would our love. As Nancy Delaney says

> While you seem to want it to be true that, were you to become a schmuck, your lover would continue to love you, you also want it to be the case that your lover would never love a schmuck.

In contrast, if love bestows value on the beloved gratuitously, regardless of their worth, then love becomes something that cannot be justified. In this sense, love is blind and it is hard to see what this valuing amounts to.

> Love is blind and lovers cannot see
> The petty follies that themselves commit.
> (*Shakespeare: Merchant of Venice*)

A fourth view sees love primarily as an emotion, something we feel, something that affects us.

> We feel love as we feel that warmth of the blood, we breathe it as we breathe the air, we carry it in ourselves as we carry our thoughts.
> (Guy de Maupassant)

To say that love is simply a feeling is hopelessly inadequate. Emotions, however, are more than feelings and include some sort of evaluation. When we are threatened, we feel fear and our emotion includes an appraisal of the danger. If love as an emotion includes some such appraisal of the beloved it takes us back to the third view of love.

A more complex view of love as an emotion would include something of the history of the lovers. Over time lovers develop an emotional interdependence so that they not only feel sad or disappointed when things go wrong for their lover but acquire a richer and more complicated set of responses. We may feel hurt when our lover is indifferent to us where other people's indifference would not trouble us. We may feel able to smile or laugh in a gentle, loving way when they are embarrassed and tease them when they are being pompous. Seeing love as a labyrinth of emotions in the context of a developing story helps to dismiss the notion of it as something that comes and goes in the way a feeling might. This organic view also accommodates change on the part of the individuals which in some cases may lead to the dissolution of that love. Because the development of a relationship over time inevitably contributes to the shaping of personality, the sudden absence of the emotional kinship may result in a loss of a sense of identity and self-worth.

Our exploration of these aspects of love has been to see if the notion of perfect love makes sense. Seen as a union of heart and mind, a perfect love would obliterate all individuality resulting in clone-like behaviour. Seen as concern, perfect love tends towards something obsessive and smothering. How many partners anxious about their beloved have been told to relax, let go, let be and make the most of the moments they have together? It is interesting to note that love as a union and love as concern do not fit easily together for the more love is seen as a union, the more love as a concern becomes self-centred and introspective.

Love as valuing includes both the appreciation of the value of a person's individuality and the bestowing of value. In both cases, it is not at all clear what perfect love would mean. To appraise someone perfectly would entail a perfect knowledge and understanding of the person and a perfect expression of their worth. We can imagine partners saying "She understands me perfectly and knows me better than I know myself." "He always compliments and encourages me." What is entailed in this perfect knowledge; a complete understanding of our history, an ability to read our minds and know exactly how we will respond? Such insight begins to feel less like love and more like psychoanalysis. Love which has as its essence and focus on the beloved seems inward-looking and distracts from the potential richness of a shared journey through life.

In our society, perfect love is often portrayed as following a particular journey: a meeting (ideally a love at first sight), a courtship, an engagement and a marriage followed by an endless happy life together. It's a picture of love portrayed in fairy tales and royal weddings and one that persists in the advertising dreams of our culture; on-line dating sites offer to find a partner matching our interests and personality, wedding planners offer the perfect day to start a happy life "til death us do part".

A stable family life, enduring friendships and lifelong commitments are to be valued and encouraged but if love is truly all we need, and if love makes the word go round we should not substitute a particular form of life for it. It makes sense to say we can be more loving, more caring, more concerned, more understanding, more honest and more trusting and that some relationships can be more personally valuable, enriching, pleasurable and satisfying, but talk of perfect love suggests an end to our exploration and a closure, rather than a springboard. Notions of perfection distort the character of love by suggesting that we are in or out of love ("she loves me, she loves me not") and travelling along a given path to a particular end. It isn't that our loves are imperfect or that they cannot be improved and deepened but that the quality of our relationships depend upon many factors; our continuing integrity and trust, our desire to share our hopes and fears, the flourishing of ourselves and our willingness to learn, none of which have a particular goal, or are ever complete. Love, as St Paul reminds us "never ends".

Place

There's a place for us,
Somewhere . .
Somewhere
We'll find a new way of living,
We'll find a way of forgiving
(Stephen Sondheim:*West Side Story)*

Human beings have always dreamt of a place where they could be happy, a perfect place of peace, security and love, a *eutopia,* a good place (from the Greek *eu* meaning good). When written as *utopia* the word means no place (from the Greek *ou* meaning not). Perhaps with this paradoxical meaning in mind, Thomas More coined the word for his island paradise. His book, written in 1516, describes a place where armies have been disbanded and work has been reduced to a minimum. While the Utopians can obtain their food from public storehouses and eat at home, most prefer to eat communally in public dining rooms, enjoying the company of others. With free health care and all needs provided money is a thing of the past and the inhabitants are invited to use their gold and silver to make chamber-pots!

Utopian visions date from the earliest times. Without giving us the political detail, the prophet Isaiah in the 8th century BCE looks to a time when

... the eyes of the blind be opened
and the ears of the deaf unstopped.
Then will the lame leap like a deer,
and the mute tongue shout for joy.
Water will gush forth in the wilderness
and streams in the desert.
The burning sand will become a pool,

> the thirsty ground bubbling springs.
> In the haunts where jackals once lay,
> grass and reeds and papyrus will grow.
> and
> they shall beat their swords into plowshares, and their spears into pruninghooks: nation shall not lift up sword against nation, neither shall they learn war any more.

Prophets, as is often said, are not fortune-tellers gazing into crystal balls, trying to predict the future but people who see the present situation clearly, criticizing and warning of the consequences that will result unless there is a change of heart and direction. Much utopian literature is also satirical and critical of contemporary life, of its technology, restrictions and laws. Dystopian (or *cacotopian* from the Greek meaning wicked) visions paint the consequences of the present trends with even more disturbing scenarios. In George Orwell's *1984*, any sense of reality for those living under the dictatorship of Oceana is destroyed through Doublethink, the power to hold and accept contradictory views at the same time, giving rise to its slogans "War is peace", "Ignorance is strength" and "Freedom is slavery". It's a telling condemnation of Stalinist Russia and Nazi Germany, warning of a future which could easily, or some would say has already, come to pass.

There is a rich variety of utopian dreams – technological, political, ecological and spiritual – which may well suggest that no one utopian dream will satisfy the diversity of human individuality. At the heart of all them is the hope of a just society where wealth and opportunity are fairly distributed and where each person enjoys the freedom to pursue his or her own desires. As a criticism of contemporary society, these imaginative visions can be powerful and motivating but as blueprints for a perfect society they fail. Perfect equality is not compatible with perfect liberty.

As an example, many utopians are city-planners and create maps for their cities with streets radiating from central resources, and identical houses with same-sized gardens but the carefully drawn plans disguise many inequalities. Some inhabitants are bound to be further than others from their place of work or the communal resources. Some will be nearer the city centre, some enjoying more sunlight than others. Equal sized gardens will not suit everyone's needs. Keen gardeners and growers will welcome a large plot of land which others will find burdensome. These may seem trivial inequalities and it may be possible to overcome them but equality goes beyond social conditions to include income, opportunity, rights, obligations and satisfaction. Finding a common definition for any one of these is impossible. Equality of income, for example, is it a flat rate for all or dependent upon work done, or levels of skill and experience?

In order to achieve the perfect society, most utopias place restrictions upon their citizens, in some cases very severe restrictions. Both More's Utopia and Plato's Republic have enslaved citizens. A further restriction comes from the boundaries of the city in that many utopias are not only geographically but demographically bounded. More has 6,000 families (each including 10 to 13 adults) in his 54 cities. Plato's Republic has 5,040 citizens. Children, however, grow into adults who marry, have offspring, grow old and become dependent. The boundaries which enabled the perfect city to function soon break down as the society evolves or else more severe restrictions are placed on the inhabitants in an attempt to shore up the boundaries.

The elements of control that are necessary to make the society function in an egalitarian way seem to assume that standardized humans inhabit them. Conflicts don't arise as everyone has the same wishes or at least any differences perfectly complement each other. If the individuals desire exactly what is imposed upon them then they have no real freedom to choose as things are the same everywhere in the utopia. If on the other hand individuals do not desire what utopia offers but submit to its rules, then again they have no real liberty as they are not able to do what they want. Isaiah Berlin, in *The Power of Ideas*, put the argument like this;

> Perfect liberty is not compatible with perfect equality. If a man is free to do anything he chooses, then the strong will crush the weak, the wolves will eat the sheep, and this puts an end to equality. If perfect equality is to be attained, then men must be prevented from outdistancing each other, whether in material or in intellectual or in spiritual achievement, otherwise inequalities will result.

For Berlin, the utopian society (achieving both perfect liberty and perfect equality) is impossible. Further, neither a perfectly egalitarian society nor a perfectly free society is desirable as both lead to a great deal of human suffering.

Berlin does not have a very positive view of human beings, asserting that left to their own devices they become wolves. It reminds us of William Golding's dystopian vision in *Lord of the Flies* where schoolboys, having survived an air crash and resorting to self-determination, descend into savagery. Perfect societies are only possible with perfect people. Indeed Thomas More makes the statement in *Utopia*.

> You can't hope to make everything perfect unless you only have perfect people to deal with – which isn't very likely for a few years yet.

If utopia is thought to be unsurpassable then, it will be argued that it is worth creating whatever the cost. Isaiah Berlin put the question: "If it's possible to attain a final solution to all human ills, then what price could be too high to pay for such a goal? In his use of the phrase "final solution", Berlin was reminding us that Hitler, Lenin, Trotsky and Mao turned utopian visions into dystopian worlds. "Our revolution" said Hitler, "is a new stage or, rather, the final stage in an evolution which will end by abolishing history". Mao's vision was equally final "When human society advances to the point where classes and states are eliminated, there will be no wars, counter-revolutionary or revolutionary, unjust or just; that will be the era of perpetual peace for mankind." Realizing such visions justified for them the slaughter of millions in wars and revolutions.

> ...gas chambers, gulag, genocide, all the monstrosities for which our century will be remembered - are the price men must pay for the felicity of future generations... (*The Proper Study of Mankind* by Isaiah Berlin)

Christians may be reminded of another utopia for which the personal cost is high.

> ...the kingdom of heaven is like a merchant seeking beautiful pearls, who, when he had found one pearl of great price, went and sold all that he had and bought it. (*Matthew 13: 45*)

Isn't the Kingdom of God not only utopia but one that is realisable on earth? After all, Christians pray in the Lord's Prayer for the kingdom to come "on earth as in heaven". It's an important concept in the teaching of Jesus and provides us with a guide for our utopian thinking.

First, the kingdom of God is not a blueprint for a utopian society. Far from laying out specific plans for a perfect way of living, many of the sixty sayings about the kingdom are parables, beginning with the words the kingdom of heaven is like . . . a sower, a merchant, ten virgins, a net, leaven. Many suggest that the kingdom is already present among, or within God's disciples.

Second, the kingdom of God, like the sayings of the prophets, challenges us to review our present circumstances and our own motives and desires. "Blessed are the poor in spirit for theirs is the kingdom of heaven" teaches Jesus in Matthew's Gospel. In Luke's Gospel the phrase is subtly but significantly different "Blessed are the poor for theirs is the kingdom of heaven." It is impossible to know which of these, if any, can be traced back to Jesus himself but for those who take these sayings to heart, they challenge their attitudes to poverty and the poverty of their resolve.

Thirdly, the kingdom is said to be both here in the present and in the future reminding us that an obsession with a blueprint for a perfect world can distract us from an appreciation of the present. In the gospel parables the kingdom breaks in like a thief in the night, unexpected and without warning. So too we need to be alert for good things breaking into our world through changing circumstances and the efforts of others.

Fourthly, the kingdom of God grows. It is like yeast in a loaf of bread, like a seed in the ground producing fruit. So many utopian visions are static with little opportunity for change. The life of society changes and grows and those who seek justice, fairness and peace will be constantly accommodating that change.

For many the association of a perfect human life with totalitarianism has led them to give up on all dreams of a better world and political engagement. The extreme suffering of ethnic cleansing, torture and brainwashing has brought about a traumatised life of hopeless despair. The meaningless of so much destruction in the name of political progress induces an apathy of indifference. From this loss of confidence in utopian visions has come what Samuel Moyn has called "The Last Utopia" – a utopian vision that doesn't rely on notions of perfection but has revitalised practical and legal human concern.

For Moyn, the emergence of the movement to protect human

rights in international law is a very recent phenomenon of the 1970s following the failure of utopian visions of the past. Others will see this has having grown gradually from a long history of resolve after conflict, including the Rights of Man discussions, the United States Declaration of Independence of the 18th century, anti-slavery campaigns, national liberation movements, establishment of the Red Cross in the 19th century, war trials and the Universal Declaration of Human Rights of the early 20th century. Our passion for human rights comes not from any utopian vision but from fear and a desire to avoid the worst evils and the intentional cruelty of systematically inflicting pain on the weak. Either way there is hope of making a difference by mounting campaigns against torture, genocide, female genital mutilation and establishing protection in law. The International Criminal Court was set up in 2002, and in 2012 sentenced the Congolese rebel Thomas Lubanga Dyilo to a total period of 14 years of imprisonment, thereby confirming the global consensus that serious violations of human rights must not go unpunished. Victims have the right to claim justice, including within processes to restore the rule of law following conflicts.

The United Nations lists amongst its achievements in the 21st century

> Success in bringing about recognition that those subjected to trafficking are victims rather than perpetrators of crime and entitled to the full range of human rights,
>
> An international framework that recognizes the challenges facing migrants and their families which guarantees their rights,
>
> A paradigm shift in the recognition of the human rights of people with disabilities, especially and crucially, their right to effective participation in all spheres of life on an equal basis with others
>
> The acknowledgement of women's rights as fundamental

human rights. Discrimination and acts of violence against women are at the forefront of the human rights discourse.

These may seem small gains when set against the inhuman atrocities that are reported every day, but they are not insignificant and begin to build a legal framework for improvement and justice.

We don't need blueprints for a perfect society. To do good in the world we need prophets who recognise the ills of our present actions and their future consequences. Utopian and dystopian visions, like the parables of the kingdom of God, can break through prejudice and indifference and sow in us seeds of hope.

End

The Lord almighty grant us a quiet night and a perfect end.

Amen.

Brethren, be sober, be vigilant; because your adversary the devil, as a roaring lion, walketh about, seeking whom he may devour: whom resist, steadfast in the faith.

The Order for Compline

As a youngster, I was always amused by this opening to the service of Compline, one of the night services of the church. Later, whenever I had to lead the service as a minster, I'd make the devil roar and prowl with great gusto. More recently, and particularly after my wife's death in 2008, my imagination is sparked by the opening phrase "grant us... a perfect end." What would be the perfect way to end our lives?

Lucy's life ended in a way typical of many people today. She suffered from Motor Neurone Disease for five years but her experience as a hospital manager and as a health visitor enabled her to anticipate her needs and prepare for them. This was a considerable help to me.

She remained lucid almost to the end of her life even though soon after the onset of the disease, she lost the power of speech. Through a speech generating machine and later, when she was unable to type, through a letterboard, she was able to communicate until the day before her death.

As a nurse and a medic, Lucy was, at a certain level, interested in the progress of the disease which she described as her "creeping paralysis". She knew how it would progress and how she would die, displaying a keenness, as a medical teacher and mentor, to support and help her young carers in understanding a disease which some had never encountered. She not only wanted to put her own affairs in order, even to the extent of planning her funeral and writing her own eulogy, but also wished to be proactive in ordering mine; given half a chance she would have sought me out another wife before she died! I wouldn't want to present this stage of her illness through rose-tinted glass; there were moments of intense anger and frustration for both of us.

As time went on and different muscles grew weaker, her breathing became more difficult. She had an oxygen mask but was never very happy wearing it and for someone with her condition it was not an easy thing to use. When the situation worsened she asked me to send for the doctor, to whom with the aid of the letterboard I was holding, she was able to spell out the problem with her breathing. The doctor, perhaps knowing Lucy was a medic, spoke a little more bluntly than he might had the patient been less professionally informed. "There is nothing I can do about that", he said. Lucy began to spell out a second message M O R P . . "Morphine", I anticipated. "Well I can give you that", said the doctor, "but it will kill you." "Yes", she said and that was the end of the conversation.

Morphine has the effect of relaxing the body so that breathing does become very much easier, and was therefore an appropriate prescription to give in such a situation but the consequence of administering the morphine was that she gradually lost consciousness. Within twenty four hours she died very peacefully and exactly in the way her consultant had described several years earlier. It's a very common scenario, but I'm quite clear in my own mind that not only did Lucy know exactly what she was asking for, but that she understood I knew it too.

Did Lucy's doctor ease her suffering, or help her to die? He did both. And what her doctor did is what doctors do every day. They help people to die peacefully and, as in Lucy's case, with the patient fully understanding what is happening. It was not euthanasia but it was a good death. Yet I would hardly describe it as the perfect end to her life.

The Litany of the church has another challenging prayer

From famine and disaster;
from violence, murder and dying unprepared,
Good Lord, deliver us.

What is it to die unprepared and therefore, presumably, fail to come to a perfect end? In medieval England, the rituals for the preparation of death were clearly defined. John Lingard, in *Antiquities of the Anglo-Saxon Church* describes the duties of the Anglo-Saxon priest.

> At the first appearance of danger, recourse was had to the ministry of the parish priest... He was bound to obey the summons and no plea but that of inability could justify his negligence...
>
> The first duty which he was bound to require from his dying disciple was the arrangement of his temporal concerns. Till provision had been made for the payment of his debts and the indemnification of those whom he had injured, it was in vain to solicit the succours of religion, but as soon as these obligations had been fulfilled the priest was ordered to receive his confession, to teach him to form sentiments of compunction and resignation, to exact from him a declaration that he died in peace with all mankind, and to pronounce over him the prayer of reconciliation.
>
> Thus prepared he might with confidence demand the Sacrament of Extreme Unction. With consecrated oil the principal parts of the body were successively anointed in the form of a cross; each unction was accompanied with an appropriate prayer and the promise of St. James was renewed, 'that the prayer of faith should save the sick man and if he be in sins they should be forgiven'
>
> The administration of the Eucharist concluded these religious rites at the termination of which the friends of the sick man ranged themselves around his bed, received the

presents which he distributed among them as memorials of his affection, and gave him the kiss of peace and bade him a last and melancholy farewell.

The importance of these rituals of dying to the believing Catholic has been dramatically portrayed in fiction. In Evelyn Waugh's *Brideshead Revisted,* there is much discussion amongst the family as to whether Lord Marchmain, a lapsed Catholic, who has returned to the family estate to die, should receive the last rites. At first, Marchmain refuses to see a priest but then later, barely conscious, near to death and unable to resist, is administered the sacrament by the priest. The family claims that the dying man is attempting to make the sign of the cross. He has achieved salvation. It has a profound effect upon the members of the family with lifelong consequences.

Whether or not we believe in the efficacy of the last rites, there are elements which we might all aspire to - having our affairs in order, making a will, sorting out our financial obligations, finding peace with ourselves and the world and saying goodbye to families and friends.

In many respects Lucy was lucky; she had good medical care and pain relief, two very confident and supportive sons and loving grandchildren. At no time did she ever express a desire to end her life or for me to end it for her and I don't know how I would have responded if she had asked. Many do, however, aspire to end their life at time of their choosing, especially when they can only see a bleak future ahead or a situation they would find unbearable. Not wanting to exist in a state in which they might be unable to communicate or do the things they love, and the desire not to "become a burden", or to be kept alive artificially, are strong motivations for people wishing to plan and even initiate the end of their lives.

Such a death is by no means an easy way out, for while the subject may be spared pain, relatives can feel hurt and excluded, protesting that they would willingly be involved in the care of their loved ones. Dignitas, the Swiss organisation which seeks to safeguard human dignity in life and in death and assists its members and others in a legally accompanied suicide, takes great care to counsel patients and members of their families. To be assisted to die, patients must be of sound judgement, and possess a minimum level of physical mobility sufficient to self-administer the drug. They must also suffer from a disease which will lead to death and / or suffer from an unendurable incapacitating disability, and / or suffer unbearable and uncontrollable pain.

Some will, through Dignitas, achieve the end they seek and die with dignity supported and surrounded by family and friends. However very many terminal patients do not fit these criteria and while they may at one time have hoped to plan the end of their life, the spread of a disease can all too quickly rob them of the physical or mental capacities needed to qualify for an assisted suicide. Even if they do, dying in a foreign country in a strange room may seem a very unsatisfactory and less than comforting proposition. These issues can arouse great passions and are hotly debated but none is guaranteed to bring our lives to a wholly satisfactory end, for while our own relationship with life ends with our death that of our family and friends continues.

A life is not contained in a single entity but is a story told in over-lapping narratives, revised and rewritten down through the generations. I have recently transcribed a series of my father's letters sent to Mum just before and during the Second World War. As they include those written during a period of time he spent in France and Germany, they provide a social comment on the life and culture of the time. On a more personal level they give an insight into their affecting relationship as it grows from the tentative approach of an "introductory note" to the warm expression of deepening affection and love in marriage. At first I felt rather voyeuristic in reading them but then decided that my mother, in deliberately passing them on to me, was in fact keen for me to read them and save them to the family archive. Later my mother spent many years looking after her father who came to live with us when I was a boy and soon after his death my father became ill prolonging her role as family carer. As I read the letters I wondered whether in bequeathing them to me, she wanted my sister and I to understand that Mum and Dad had once been young themselves and full of the enthusiasm and optimism of burgeoning love.

This challenged me to see my parents in a new light and reassess my feelings towards them. I now regret the many opportunities I had when they were alive to get to know them better and find ways of expressing my love and appreciation for the sacrifices they had made for me.

The story of our lives continues to evolve after our death, and, if we are lucky may influence and challenge others. We may, however, be amongst those described bleakly by the writer of Ecclesiasticus: "and some there be, which have no memorial; who are perished, as though they had never been; and are become as though they had never been born; forgotten with no memorial."

The bittersweet nature of life and death and the inconclusive nature of our passing rob the idea of a perfect end of any meaning. Our efforts should be put into providing the very best palliative care, learning to live with and embrace the dying, respecting their wishes and the hopes and fears of relatives. Those who don't have the luxury of preparation, who die suddenly, sometimes in the most violent, brutal and horrific manner, and die before their life has really begun must be honoured by us through a search for justice and truth, and in a search for the hope of a meaningful future for their families.

But what of heaven? Isn't perfection seen only after this life in the celestial city? Are not Christians called home to the consummation, joy and worship of paradise? The Catechism of the Catholic Church, quoting *Lumen Gentium*, states

> The Church... will receive her perfection only in the glory of heaven, when will come the time of the renewal of all things. At that time, together with the human race, the universe itself, which is so closely related to man and which attains its destiny through him, will be perfectly re-established in Christ.

Depictions of heaven whether visual or imagined can be extremely vivid. They may be extremely comforting to some but they are all fictional since talk of heaven is metaphorical, even the use of the word "after" in the phrase life after death. There are few descriptions of heaven in the bible; our final end is "in God". This is not something happening after death because we are in life in God, the God in "whom we live and move and have our being".

The Christian path has often been regarded as a journey from earth to heaven. Yet Christians follow Christ who, in the words of the Christmas carol *Once in Royal David's city,* "came down to earth from heaven". Paul in his letter to the church at Philippi, perhaps quoting an earlier Christian hymn, put it rather more fully:

> Let this mind be in you, which was also in Christ Jesus: Who, being in the form of God, thought it not robbery to be equal with God: But made himself of no reputation, and took upon him the form of a servant, and was made in the likeness of men: And being found in fashion as a man, he humbled himself, and became obedient unto death, even the death of the cross.

We must begin to see our journey into God as one which immerses us in our humanity and an acceptance of the human condition.

It is not altogether surprising then that we have seen the same dynamic in our search for beauty, goodness, justice and love. Plato, the early Greek philosopher, envisaged a world of perfect forms which gave rise to the imperfect copies of everything in our world. This isn't the way we now see things. Creating beauty is not achieved by copying a formula or seeking to transcend the material world but by returning again to humankind and to the community of performers, artists and audiences, revising, recreating and improving our work. Our search for goodness led us to embrace the inevitable conflict of duties, wrestle with the all the complexities of action and to risk spontaneous responses when called upon, and dare to confront failure and abuse for our efforts.

In a search for love, there is no end to our exploration, no end to our growth or commitment and once again we find ourselves on an incarnational road. "Love", as St Paul says, "never ends" but invites us to return again and again to the integrity of our relationships, our hopes and fears and to an ever deepening commitment. So too in our hopes for a better society, there is no blueprint for those working for the kingdom of God, only an ever deepening engagement with the issues that can improve people's lives, challenging prejudice in ourselves and others.

CHRISTIAN ALTERNATIVE

Christian Alternative
THE NEW OPEN SPACES

Throughout the two thousand years of Christian tradition there have been, and still are, groups and individuals that exist in the margins and upon the edge of faith. But in Christianity's contrapuntal history it has often been these outcasts and pioneers that have forged contemporary orthodoxy out of former radicalism as belief evolves to engage with and encompass the ever-changing social and scientific realities. Real faith lies not in the comfortable certainties of the Orthodox, but somewhere in a half-glimpsed hinterland on the dirt track to Emmaus, where the Death of God meets the Resurrection, where the supernatural Christ meets the historical Jesus, and where the revolution liberates both the oppressed and the oppressors.

Welcome to Christian Alternative... a space at the edge where the light shines through.
If you have enjoyed this book, why not tell other readers by posting a review on your preferred book site. Recent bestsellers from Christian Alternative are:

Bread Not Stones
The Autobiography of An Eventful Life
Una Kroll
The spiritual autobiography of a truly remarkable woman and a history of the struggle for ordination in the Church of England.
Paperback: 978-1-78279-804-0 ebook: 978-1-78279-805-7

The Quaker Way

A Rediscovery

Rex Ambler

Although fairly well known, Quakerism is not well understood. The purpose of this book is to explain how Quakerism works as a spiritual practice.

Paperback: 978-1-78099-657-8 ebook: 978-1-78099-658-5

Blue Sky God

The Evolution of Science and Christianity

Don MacGregor

Quantum consciousness, morphic fields and blue-sky thinking about God and Jesus the Christ.

Paperback: 978-1-84694-937-1 ebook: 978-1-84694-938-8

Celtic Wheel of the Year

Tess Ward

An original and inspiring selection of prayers combining Christian and Celtic Pagan traditions, and interweaving their calendars into a single pattern of prayer for every morning and night of the year.

Paperback: 978-1-90504-795-6

Christian Atheist

Belonging without Believing

Brian Mountford

Christian Atheists don't believe in God but miss him: especially the transcendent beauty of his music, language, ethics, and community.

Paperback: 978-1-84694-439-0 ebook: 978-1-84694-929-6

Compassion Or Apocalypse?
A Comprehensible Guide to the Thoughts of René Girard
James Warren
How René Girard changes the way we think about God and the Bible, and its relevance for our apocalypse-threatened world.
Paperback: 978-1-78279-073-0 ebook: 978-1-78279-072-3

Diary Of A Gay Priest
The Tightrope Walker
Rev. Dr. Malcolm Johnson
Full of anecdotes and amusing stories, but the Church is still a dangerous place for a gay priest.
Paperback: 978-1-78279-002-0 ebook: 978-1-78099-999-9

Do You Need God?
Exploring Different Paths to Spirituality Even For Atheists
Rory J.Q. Barnes
An unbiased guide to the building blocks of spiritual belief.
Paperback: 978-1-78279-380-9 ebook: 978-1-78279-379-3

The Gay Gospels
Good News for Lesbian, Gay, Bisexual, and Transgendered People
Keith Sharpe
This book refutes the idea that the Bible is homophobic and makes visible the gay lives and validated homoerotic experience to be found in it.
Paperback: 978-1-84694-548-9 ebook: 978-1-78099-063-7

The Illusion of "Truth"

The Real Jesus Behind the Grand Myth

Thomas Nehrer

Nehrer, uniquely aware of Reality's integrated flow, elucidates Jesus' penetrating, often mystifying insights – exposing widespread religious, scholarly and skeptical fallacy.

Paperback: 978-1-78279-548-3 ebook: 978-1-78279-551-3

Do We Need God to be Good?

An Anthropologist Considers the Evidence

C.R. Hallpike

What anthropology shows us about the delusions of New Atheism and Humanism.

Paperback: 978-1-78535-217-1 ebook: 978-1-78535-218-8

Fingerprints of Fire, Footprints of Peace

A Spiritual Manifesto from a Jesus Perspective

Noel Moules

Christian spirituality with attitude. Fourteen provocative pictures, from Radical Mystic to Messianic Anarchist, that explore identity, destiny, values and activism.

Paperback: 978-1-84694-612-7 ebook: 978-1-78099-903-6

Readers of ebooks can buy or view any of these bestsellers by clicking on the live link in the title. Most titles are published in paperback and as an ebook. Paperbacks are available in traditional bookshops. Both print and ebook formats are available online.